# COMPACT DISC PAGE AND BAND INFORMATION

MMO CD 3328
MMO Cass. 8008

## LAUREATE SERIES CONTEST SOLOS
### ADVANCED LEVEL FOR FLUTE

| Band No. Complete Version | | Band No. Minus Flute | Page No. |
|---|---|---|---|
| 1 | *Handel:* Sonata No. 2 in G minor: | | |
| | - Adagio | 7 | 6 |
| 2 | - Presto | 8 | 7 |
| | - Presto ( Slow Version) | 9 | |
| 3 | *Telemann:* Suite in A minor - II "Les Plaisirs" | 10 | 8 |
| 4 | *Henze:* Sonatine I | 11 | 10 |
| | Sonatine I (Slow Version) | 12 | 10 |
| 5 | *Quantz:* Concerto in G Major | 13 | 12 |
| 6 | Concerto in G Major (Slow Version) | 14 | 12 |
| | - Tuning Notes - | | |

MMO CD 3328

Printed in Canada

# LS LAUREATE SERIES

## FLUTE MUSIC BOOK

**TUNING**
Before the piano accompaniment begins you will hear four tuning notes, followed by a short scale and another tuning note. This will enable you to tune your instrument to the record.

MMO CD 3328

# PERFORMANCE GUIDE
## COMMENTARY BY MURRAY PANITZ

### HANDEL
#### Sonata No. 2 in G Minor: Adagio and Presto

It is most important to sustain notes their full value. Handel style suffers if notes are too short or clipped. Work for a full, round tone. Even when there are dots over the notes, there must be a feeling of deep support. Listen carefully to the accompaniment; there are many little conversations between the piano and the flute. Notice the pattern in measures 8 and 9:

One of the most important things you can develop is a concept of sound. It is not difficult to create a noise; to create a *musical* noise is the task. Keep working until your noise is a pleasant one! If you just played the notes, you would have only a part of the components in the musical totality. Try for variety. Remember, you would tire of ice cream alone. You must have a well-balanced diet made up of rhythm, sound, and structure.

Even though the Presto moves at a fast pace, you must be sure that the second notes in slurred passages are not shortened. They must extend all the way through the beat. The section beginning in measure 14 may tempt you to shorten every other note. Don't fall into that trap. When you play the trills, try to maintain the quality of the bottom note. I have often heard false trills, which fall somewhere between the two notes being trilled. Concentrate on your embouchure, and forget the fluttering of your fingers. Remember that the trill is a vehical of expression, and let the style of the music help you decide how to play it!

### TELEMANN
#### "Les Plaisirs" from the Suite in A Minor

This piece is a fine study in articulation. There is much *non-legato* playing which requires a certain bite to the tone, but length to the note. Play the mordent in measure 21 quickly. Remember that embellishments must stay within the structure of the music. The Trio is usually played in a slightly faster tempo. The repeated eighth note patterns must be made exciting so that they are not merely repetitive. Because the flute is capable of such florid ornamentation, it is important to look for the melodic interest hidden in all the embellishments!

### HENZE
#### Sonatine, 1st Movement

The Henze Sonatine is a fine combination of smooth curving lines and angularity, interspersed with long unaccompanied passages. It is important to establish the mood with the very first notes. After the vibrant beginning, the *dolce* in measure 20 provides an opportunity for contrast. It may be helpful if you create imaginary characters. You might pretend that the hero enters at the beginning. Then, at the *dolce,* the heroine enters, pleading fervently! Although absolute music doesn't tell a story, a device of this kind may help you give the music more impact.

Watch the phrasing in the cut-time section. When you have two slurred notes, the second note must not be clipped short. Study the articulation marked, and try to outline the pattern of the phrase. Remember that repeated notes help to build tension. The dynamics are bold and full of color. If you play with audacity you will create a most interesting piece.

### QUANTZ
#### Concerto in G Major: 1st Movement (Allegro)

This is a charming piece in the old bravura style. Be aware of the slightly different moods: the opening theme, second theme, development and recapitulation. The florid passages need a little inflection so that they have a forward thrust. The articulation in this edition is very good. The slurred notes add to the variety. Be careful not to clip the second note of a two note slur. The three note groupings will be very difficult if you don't give them a little lift.

The trills are difficult from the standpoint of rhythm. You should try to differentiate between the trill followed by two sixteenths, and the trill followed by two thirty-seconds. (This is easier said than done!) Be sure the note the trill begins on is heard clearly, especially in ascending passages such as the one in measure 33.

(All through the baroque and classic periods composers wrote long lines of notes with no breathing places. You will need to find the note of least importance, omit it, and take your breath in its place. The important thing is to keep the *thought* going without interruption.)

The interval on the first beat of measure 65 is very difficult. It may be simplified in this way:

The repeated notes in the section beginning in measure 72 need a forward drive. Do not try to play the low notes in measures 76 and 83 too softly; the flute must be heard above the accompaniment. Practice carefully, and you will have a piece which displays the flute in all its silvery brilliance!

*Murray W. Panitz*

# SONATA NO. 2 IN G MINOR

♪ = 66 (2'19")

G. F. HANDEL

MMO CD 3328

MMO CD 3328

# SUITE IN A MINOR

## II "Les Plaisirs"

G. P. TELEMANN
Trans. by John Wummer

♩ = 126 (3'23")

*D. C. Les Plaisirs al Fine*

# SONATINE

## I

HANS WERNER HENZE

MMO CD 3328

# CONCERTO IN G MAJOR

## I

♩ = 116 (4'23")
♩ = 76 (6'11")

JOHANN JOACHIM QUANTZ
Revised by John Wummer

Allegro

MMO CD 3328

14

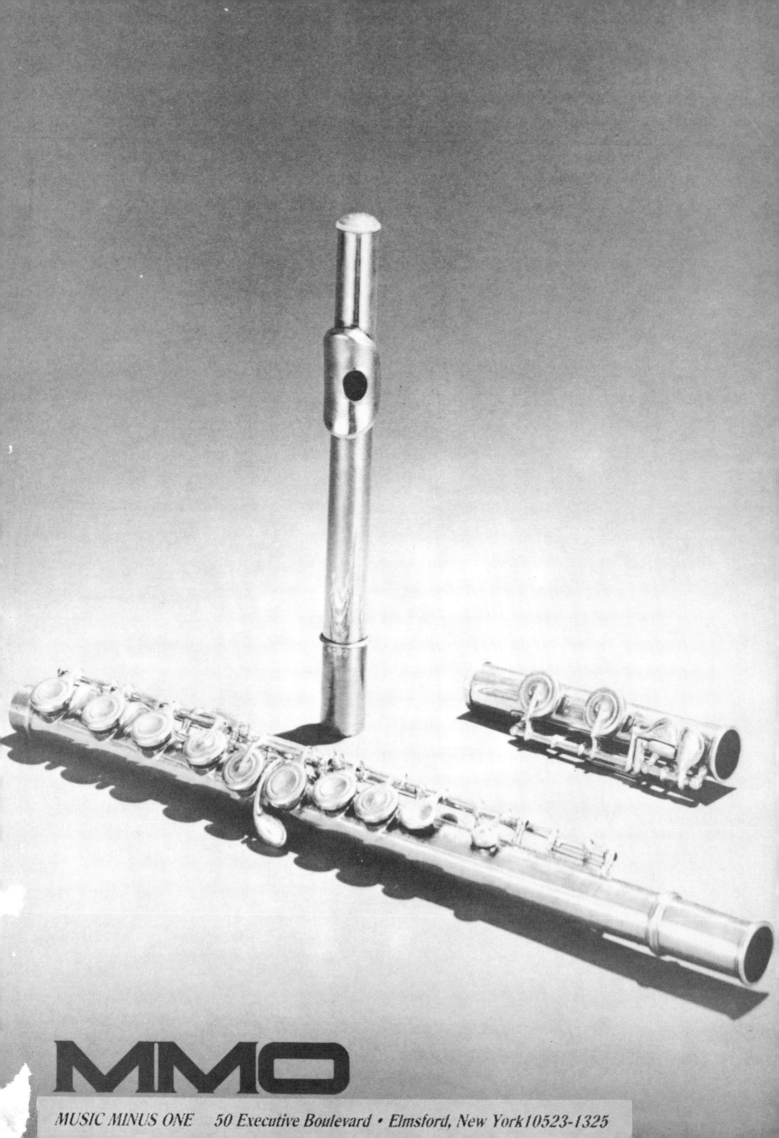